Line to Curve

Anna Reckin

Line to Curve

Shearsman Books

First published in the United Kingdom in 2018 by
Shearsman Books
50 Westons Hill Drive
Emersons Green
BRISTOL
BS16 7DF

Shearsman Books Ltd Registered Office
30–31 St. James Place, Mangotsfield, Bristol BS16 9JB
(this address not for correspondence)

www.shearsman.com

ISBN 978-1-84861-580-9

Contents

IV Sees

I

Making

Couture

Make a fall
and calculate
its break,
its swing, its
outwards roll –

shell or a skim, stretch
gather
fold, see

how contour pulls at edges:

arch of a wave's back

arabesque of trailing foam

from line to curve

thread : cloth : clothe

Her glass-green beads –

sharp as daisies

apples, tinfoil, cans of

cling-wrapped   fish

meat

real & simulated voices

scanning fruit

lightbulbs   milk

making morning out of

plate-glass

evening

– her yellow, sunshine dress

Sounds here like sea air

are held in suspension. Flap, drop, a laugh. Quietly, footsteps. Something dragged, and voices – 'How long you staying?' 'Twenty past, now' – rise clear to the surface, are re-absorbed. Clean-swept, footsteps, a radio three stalls down. Sun brightens, and the noises sharpen, pick up pace. Teaspoons & china, chair-scrape, 'Hey!' Open and shut, footsteps. Breeze catches some, turns some away. Murmurs, laughter, a gentle swell, between the rows – and beyond. 'About 40 years ago.' The calm of inconsequence.

Making Maia, Ash Wednesday afternoon

Vermelho for the scarf, so what about the ribbon for the waist? Clock ticks, the soft-soft whirr of the sewing machine; something falls in the hearth (clever sticks, no grate). Even so, the logs keep their shape. Over straight-straight arms and tied at the back, skirts ballooning. Over across & across again. Good Friday wrappings. He'll be more than life-size on the night, high up, leaning outwards. Blue-and-white china on the dresser, shelves edged with lace. *Hoje*, don't eat meat. Start on a new one – hidden, near the join, under white muslin underthings, two tiny bumps. 'Look,' slyly, 'She has breasts!' Needle needs filling again. Hand around – who sees the best?

Queijo

heart's squeeze

um pouco

little pans, on a table

This one

is made of wood:

round edges, grained
'tilting slightly'

for shaping

– cord, card, curdle

a pile of purple filaments

winter's chill   a focus

by hand

Adufe

held so one corner

points

down

like the back
of a shawl

∨

juggle (rest)

one side   beat

one side   on the other

palm of the hand   a flap of the fingers

make the seeds / stones jump

between

∨

Do you first see the fields?

or the paths (stone-cobbled,
between stone walls)?

It's at the cross-roads, in darkness

       Our Lady meets

               O Nosso Senhor

           V

                  mesh

    angles

Larga

Technically, a square
    but sometimes, especially in the villages – where roads leave off their making-strait, rest awhile, swill outwards

                            t
                     s   a
                            r

            on an anyhows slope. Rainwater run-off, possibly a view

And a monument. Slender pillar, more or less centred. A globe, a cross, weather-eaten, on a pedestal

                        stony focus   against
                                        which

Parquetry

Hair, rock, lettuce, head, tongue. Bulges in
lattice knit. Cross-grain rebuttals, ink-thin.

A head of lettuce, a neck of lamb.

Joints' angles, all in one plane. Imbricate
sounds but isn't right.

Locked, in the fashion of a small park.

Like furniture

Herringbones downward. Mood is [pause]
lively. Lilac and lino, foliage off-cuts, fur.
Clear soft yellow next a magenta, a cyan
(blue-green) cast. Fresh.

A can't eat tongue, a tie, a tenon. Farm and
factory, neck-tie bias

Fading flattens the latch

Darks in the central passage   Bigger
hook

II

from The Jade Album

word   temple

                [   ]

poem

                    – sounds the same as stone

Bi

A round disc with a hole at its centre

Think of it as another kind of pendant   space in the middle a juncture for

$$- \,|\, -$$

crossed threads

> as in the Lady's banner, below
> the little platform – under the
> bar of the T – where she's
> bent over her stick, servants
> in front and behind; here
> threads are
> dragon-coils…

to be hung (in life)

to be draped (in death)

vertical slice

abstract from weave

drilling makes $- \,|\, -$

a perfect circle

'Altered'

the catalogue says. Green glow gone, translucence
changed to bone-white opacity

raw to cooked, pink

flesh to white meat

food, or fixative?

– like a pot, you'd say, or ivory –

fire or fume?

soul's sustenance *and* lodging place

Kidneys

are *zang*, 'storage'. Think grain, earthly goods [and those dancing-girls,
those troupes of musicians rendered (finally) in clay]   wishes, intentions laid by

stored against –   warehouse and factory] Controlling

fear]
They also produce bone marrow,

Ground up to be eaten, to procure immortality. The better the stone,
the more efficacious the potion.

are where will-power's housed

Huan

A circle, like a bi, *but with the central hole much larger*

       Returning is not the same as going home,
         a blur, a journey to sojourn, a step back-
         wards, a sometime when

                  points got switched,
                  one layer further over

                           go back

– the better to leap

        or not   no more than

                answer's equivalence

Squared spirals tessellate 'responds' over and over; each one with

                □

kou [mouth] opening at the centre

Hanging down

– Why does it matter?

– That they're hanging? It's the sound –

– When they break?

– When they knock against each other, as the wearer moves through
the room. Or when they're strung on a wooden frame, tapped with
ivory, say, to make music. Graduated, all in strict order

*etiquette of tinkling chimes Stones
obstructing flowing plucked ripples, scale
silken strings*

– What if they fall? If the thread snaps? Or someone cuts it?
Or it rots away?

rungs rules

– They'll be silent a while. Laid out in a tray on a stall of curios;
hidden away in a drawer; in a glass box, with labels; numbers inked
on their sides

Or left underground. Disarticulated, flat, in scattered piles

smooth and glossy

      and soft, *it says* like benevolence;   fine, compact and strong like intelligence;   angular, **but not sharp and cutting** *the knives and the daggers purely ceremonial*   like *righteousness*;   **hanging down (in beads)** as if it would fall to the ground *if it did, it would shatter* like propriety;   when struck, **yielding a note clear and prolonged**, yet terminating abruptly, like music;   gilded chimes on a wooden frame   its flaws not concealing its beauty, nor its beauty concealing its flaws,   *it says* like loyalty

'soft' is the rubble edge when broken – and careful lest it crumble further (Joins can be masked with metal collars, then hinged)

                   Takes the hit. Takes the hint

Brush-pot

Shine is from inside:

           neg-snowy masses limn, load

      tree-branches, roof-edges

                delineate rock contours

            in successive   [painterly]

                       rings

   the winding bank of a stream, a small lantern

     summer shapes in wintry suspension

                  stone acting on light

Raft cup

is a pool in the palm of your hand, bowl on a writing-desk:

rhinoceros horn
/ to wood / to stone
/ to a branch with blossom on it

step down, shelf by curving shelf, wash
the dust from your feet / the ink from your brush –

is a pool on the upper surface of a blossoming cherry branch:
at the stern / base of the horn / where the branch meets the trunk
'caramel-russet' petals and stamens
carved face-out into 'the skin of the jade '

a push at boulder's limit]

is a way to reach back: –

Small mountain lyric

Old man keeps on
                westward, the boy
                at his side with a branch
                of surprising peach

      they go on up the winding steps, past pines, past tile-roofed
terraces, platforms

                                  peaks, abysses
                                  waterfalls

                                  a desktop
                                  boulder, on which –

      ground, abraded, turned
      & ground again, sand,
      water, drills, wheels
      'crystallise' mountain, valley, steps, falls

                                    where now, still climbing
                                  upwards, boy
                                  old man

                                  branch of flowering peach

III

Looks

Look, it's dark red

one way, green

the other,

  sullen &

springtime, aqua,

lilac, pink, and

one small slot

of sky-clear

blue.

Geometry's tasks

are secret; meantime

let the eye make

lines, watch

forms emerge

at different distances,

cross-check tone,

hue, saturation

see how imagined

shadows give a fixed perspective

                        – out there, where you are

Colour process (Americana)

Red pulls the composition around it   Minneapolis
cyan, magenta, black, rainslick
on wet pavement, stoplight
in midtown blur

         Yellow's time: St Louis

                that sixties sky (old stock),
                peach-white concrete wall
                ballast for ultra
                -marine

         backlit

                and vanishing

Lake-fog hides both ends of the street   Grand Marais
(resort town visit, winter; I'm lost already)

         from the beach – summertime –   Duluth
         blots out shimmer; a new
         radiant blankness
         they swim into, out
         of, disappear
         behind

Green's

                                                   Buffalo

     recessions:

Niagara's backslide west   cross-

                              continental

       (pressed water, glass
       at the lip of the fall)
           pane in section

          less fugitive, more / mere
                   [leaves' disclosures]

                            stain

Or the edge of a wood

From sunlit

      into dark-

            green darkness, ground on which

    small white, springtime, starry –

        Flora

        and blowsy, gauze-clad Chloris, clumsy bloom

        across her mouth, her sideways gaze a slide

        of picture plane, mutually embracing Graces,

                    the youth

      with wings at his heels

but I ignore the figures (gods,
girls, fruit-laden trees)

  – field at my back, I'm eyeing the verge:

            pale stems, etiolate, in half-shade

Climbing down

hardest is that first

getting out

      'twixt pitch and rock-

              a-bye

risk's

              / opportunities

/ risks

          just say, unforeseeable

closed systems

        sky-boat landing

          – you have to hoik yourself out   and

              down

                  down

             down again

branch by branch –

              get where

              you can jump

              to leaf-bare

             ground

Saxifrage: another sort of a song

Leaves shaped like kidneys, and
in clusters along the stem

or near the base, bulbils
like little shiny stones

(breakage is
on the inside)

flower-spikes spring
from rosettes, brisk

cress-green, with
many daughters; there

where water collects, leaflitter,
the beginnings
of soil.

Doesn't split. Finds
the already-cracks
                grows there

By the side of the lane

fine as fingering

lace-making's

lost stitches

kirtle over under-

things

a fall

a   way

Shook
(*Fraxinus excelsior*)

                                        sh k;
                                        sh k;
                                  sh k;

            springtime, still hanging
        dull brown
bundles   delicate
                             parched
            after-
            leaf-fall
            dull. ash-
            en

                        sh k;
                        sh k;
                  sh k;

                  like and unlike

                                      sh -ck
                                  sh -ck

                                          sh -ck

                  blackened, shrivelled
                        leaves,
                  shrunken
                                      hanging
                                      down

                        as if
                        scorch-
                            ed

dead-dull
seeds
waiting for
    wind's
    skirl:

               sh-kin   -sh-kin

Spins like

sycamore:

such tents

he says,

(dark birds against the sky

thickening, deepening, blackening

structure to

make the

loved the

movement

scatter of sparks, little tongues

& more   & more

o'er-canopy)

or hum of murmuring bees

Sunflower field, with pheasants

What persists: in amongst gaunt stems,
flashes of red, mottled rustle. Opposing spirals
arc into points. The still smoke of trees.

Near-parallels

unsupported····················(poor

··summer)

··amongst these

··thin

grasses

and ox-eye

··s t e m s

··like cables

··running

··across

··from rosette

··stake-outs

heartsease··reverts to a

··c r e e p i n g

··habitat

tattered

··bindweed

··a ladder

··for snails

Walking among the pillars

of the Great Mosque   in a forest / on a chessboard
/ among the sparkling white stones of a military cemetery

the view alters with each step, a smooth stream of new alignments. After a while – correction for dizziness? – change happens in little rushes. Following the landslide, a trickle of pebbles, tiles settling in the kaleidoscope's cylinder

in the courtyard outside, orange trees in square tubs

[boxed grove]

keep moving

Looks out

        onto a solid mass of green. London plane trees tumble the length of the glass. Look down to street level, and the trunks are surrounded by railings. Trees and iron – belt and braces. But the leaves billow out over the spikes: froth of lace over a corset.

fichu fixed with tiny pins

The gates are locked at dusk.

This is how I imagine if / memories those gardens

– intricate green sudden
enclosed in stone & sun-baked clay. Scratch of leaves on pavement,
scent of orange rind, a faint dry echo. Branches stretch from trunks
arranged in rows. Pieces of water in rectangular shapes. A place the
birds come, where they perch, gulfed, in the city.

IV

Sees

Inverse

You've heard of linear – this is backwards

                            base over precariously
                                balancing
                                   tip

a d u s t i n g

      of sandalwood, c r u m b l i n g l e a t h e r, e x o t i c p a p e r s

lifts from an overhang of mosses

musks, incense, amber   nostalgia –

lily, lily

                   carnation   among the

    rose

     heart   paeony

        iris   fountains

             finest

    ache

                petit   mind's

                        -grain   sharps

slides over the door-sill,

  top to tail

Sweet cool

zinc buckets on a North Sydney street, Iceland poppies

    – sub-arctic dazzles, the plantsman says; for scent
    Champagne Bubbles or Meadow Pastels Mixed
    sillage of cools about a round table in a bare (rental) room
    'usually will not survive hot, humid summers'

winter heliotrope, *Petasites fragrans*, November this year – early
    almond and vanilla from amongst the flat-hat leaves
    has outlasted the destruction of the hawthorn hedge

        piercing aromatic

                unexpected again

Gather

gets split:

folds stitched and stuck || glassy mass searingly still

puntil   a spine

What happened to the armfuls of lavender from the 'landscaped' grounds
near the bridge?

– haze that rises with the sun on it, and again, in winter rain, now it's cut –

opens up, full

of breath

(splay of stalks in a vase

ESSENTIAL

aerial

perspecti**v**es,   blues

e

Swiss haze

n

or sun-warme**d**

y**e**llow,   Sicilian

rose

VOLATILES

What did the orange gain

when it lost its 'n'? Orotundity and foreignness – an orange is rounder than a *naranja*. It announces its roundness at the very beginning, out loud in black type: O.

But the 'n' didn't just drop off and fall away, a curl of peel. It slid across into negative space, no-man's land, the indefinite article. There it is, in the middle: empty vessel without so much as an outline around it.

You can't throw a circle off-balance, but a painting needs a tipping movement. Something to set the eye rolling, ball on a see-saw. Teeter-totter, the clatter of utensils. Cutting-board, and the knife's an indicator. Spin it like a needle and see whose heart it points to.

Not many murder stories happen in kitchens, despite all the knives, the opportunities. Or maybe they're disembodied – the murders, I mean. Acid, or the ones that slowly boil away until the pan's burnt dry. Spices whose oils evanesce into the atmosphere...

the vanishing's the point.

Fish

A few hours after dawn, under a bridge in the middle of the city, a wooden rowing-boat, with two fishermen in it. Downstream is the outlet from the printworks, where the swans gather in a rush of warm water; upstream the corrugated cardboard factory, a choking smell of damp paper. Along here, the river's shut in, with straight-sided banks and paved paths, squared off like a canal. I would never expect fish to be here. I would think that they would stay in the greener shady places where the river edges what were once water-meadows (sand and gravel still), now playing-fields.

That night I dream of the fish in the river. The river's course has straightened, blocked off into a long narrow pool: a tank in a Mughal miniature. The city walls are smooth and high, fortified, with watchtowers, and the buildings crowd up against them: towers, domes and minarets. It's after dark, and a single fish hangs in the water, gleaming in the night-time stone.

'Untitled'
(oil on canvas, early twentieth-century)

Gentle slope to an invisible shoreline

                                     lawn, hedges, flower-beds

                                     yachts, blue sea

                  mid-distance, above scarlet geraniums

                  three or maybe four (the brushwork

                  is impressionistic, indistinct)   bird-

                  cages, on tall

                  stands; within

                            a blur of

                            white

                        'for an airing'

Dungeness

I

no fences,

not *The Last of England*: his doubtful face, her fearful one, the child's
fingers glimpsed in the curl of the shawl

    nothing to stop anyone walking in, any time

The coast road becomes The Parade, but the only promenade is over the
sands, through wavering channels, to the sea

          creaking timbers, spray, the cries of gulls
             – fade-in, fade-out, vignetted –

II

rose, and gorse,

    stones, and water, and light

III

the danger signs on the map are stamped all the way out to sea

not

[the friendly lights]

an edge   This

is the centre of some

circle

back of London

tangent

lean-to, makeshift,

Britannia   FREE HOUSE

hunkered down amid the shingle

IV

To the south, old sea-cliffs, now inland, greened. During the war, the sea-walls were breached, the levels re-flooded; against invasion

Out in the bay

|
|
|

                                                – reflection standing –

gash in the sky

|
                                             grapple &
|
                                                   tide-sweep
|

enActs a

                  star-still

                        H o v e r i n g

Don't become

the tid**A**l object

flotsam

aestheti**C**

,   wh**E**re

Dust lies, it attenuates, wrung wash-

rag

p a t h o s

;   make a

p**I**cture   :

Sisyphus pushing a ball of feathers

,   *they*

find the breeze

s c **A**t te r   quick

as

catch

can

63

Whelk

easier to draw a broken shell

than a whole one

break's edge

follows the contour

(in section

it's ribbed,

cut-away's

slant on

nested

white volutes

smaller &   close-

er. They

speak to

one a-

[not-

her]

Lollylob

throat-blot, glo'al

-scene:

sax swag

-gers upward   diAg'nal

coat-hook   'Try to re-

LA-A-X'   sez

SHUT yr   gob-not
                          heard-but

                                                seen-nnN

In plain sight

pattern's call, recall

rung

fret

strut

stripe

across & thru & beyond

a jug of flowers

cartwheels of cow-parsley, ferny foliage, teasel
head & fine grasses poised over the edge
of a table that gleams as it nears the window:
its pale-shadowy trees

and the little chair in the corner, and the
unfinished painting on the opposite wall,
flowers a white mass on a blue background –

window- and door-frame

bead, skirtings and floor-boards

diagonal of
shawl's fringe

[the bars at the end of the bed]

and the subtle syntax of shadows: light, dark, lighter still

    hard and soft edges

        You *think* you're looking –

In her arms

I

In her arms

                  she says,

feels it in her arms

                 parens

)

      (

         embrace

           – loves a frame:

                 knot drops out of a plank, the squint

                 between trees, in the angle

                 of a branch

                 eye on its side, upright

                 conch

in her *arms*

the reach from the ball of the shoulder
through elbow, wrist, to finger-tip

not a squeeze but a pull

feel the drawing through —

II

And pouring:

tilts the tin   with one or
both hands – floor
takes the weight

when the white is fully
charged with red /with pale-
straw yellow   before any
drops

(wound sluices itself)

paint thinned, to stain

one thing laps into another

all spaces are colour fields

III

So large

     you could get lost in it

         array

        as if you could walk through its dunes

         sand   sun   sky

        hunker down out of the wind

a reverie

      some details vanish when you get up close

                 wipe-marks, splash-trails

      edges, even

IV

sink

      calm, into that off-centre blue

                    that pellucid green

    notice, along the way

                        where awash ends

        oil-haloes

      cloud-soak

            liquid discriminations

V

The view a borrowed one
end of a grassy alley, a lighthouse, something
coming up on the horizon   snail
seen over the leaf it's bending

Notes

p 14 'Making Maia' is set in a backroom behind a shop in a village in Portugal. The women are making little dolls called *marafonas*, which are carried in a particular procession in the spring, but also sold all year round as good-luck charms and souvenirs. *Vermelho* is 'red'.

p 15 '*Queijo*' means cheese; the cheese-making described here uses the heads of cardoon thistles rather than animal rennet.

p 16 The *adufe* is a square tambourine or drum, traditionally played by women in north-east and central Portugal.

pp 19 & 65 'Parquetry' and 'Lollylob' are inspired by artwork by Robert Filby, part of the Obverse collaboration.

pp 22-32 The poems in the Jade Album section are taken from a longer project taking as its theme Chinese jade as a material (jadeite and nephrite) and as carved artefact. Some of the pieces described here are objects that might be found on a scholar's desk in imperial China; others (for example, the *huan* and the *bi*) are probably associated with ancient rituals.

p 35 'Look, it's dark red' is inspired by Mary Mellors' relief *Video Avian*.

pp 42-44 'Spins like' collages (in the italicised words) Coleridge. This and 'Shook' were produced in response to environmental artist Liz McGowan's project *Murmuration*, working with sycamore keys and included in *Flight*, an exhibition at the Greenhouse Gallery, Norwich, in 2014.

p 53 'Inverse' is an imagined perfume where the notes conventionally used for the base are transposed to the top, forming a kind of lintel. The relationship between base and top notes in a perfume is often presented in terms of a pyramidal structure.

p 55 'Gather' makes reference to glass- and book-making.

p 56 'Essential' plays on the sense of volatile as a flying creature; the poem was produced for the *Pollen Path* exhibition at the Greenhouse Gallery, Norwich in 2013. See http://www.paratext.co.uk/indexto-issue-2 for sonic and visual paratext, including the relevant poems by Emily Dickinson.

p 62 'Out in the bay' is a poem of the English South Coast, referencing (amongst other things) 18th-century anti-smuggling legislation.

p 66 'In plain sight' is based partly on Eric Ravilious's watercolour *Ironbridge Interior* (1941).

p 68 'In her arms' is inspired by paintings by Helen Frankenthaler and includes quotes from her writing.

Acknowledgements

Some of these poems, or earlier versions of them, appeared in the following magazines; my thanks to their editors: *Long Poem Magazine*, Linda Black and Lucy Hamilton; *Poetry Wales*, Zoë Skoulding and Nia Davies; *Tears in the Fence*, David Caddy; *Molly Bloom*, Aidan Semmens; *Brittle Star*, Jacqueline Gabbitas and Martin Parker; *Yellow Field*, Edric Mesmer; *Datableed*, Nell Perry and Juha Virtanen; *para-text*, Laura Elliott and Angus Sinclair.

'Queijo' first appeared as part of the discussion in 'Milk and Thistles', an essay in *In Their Own Words: Contemporary Poets on Their Poetry*, edited by Helen Ivory and George Szirtes (Salt, 2012).

'What did the Orange Gain' was first produced and published as part of the Dreaming Paintbrush project, based on paintings by Geoffrey Robinson and funded by Hampshire County Council.

'Don't become' was a contribution to the Dawdle project at SPACE, Hackney, 2012, curated by Gareth Bell-Jones.

'Small mountain lyric' was first published in 2013 as a broadside by Fewer and Further Press, edited by Jess Mynes.

My thanks for insightful commentary from Harriet Tarlo, Frances Presley, Richard Lambert, Sandra Guerreiro and Julia Webb.

My thanks too to the artists whose work has inspired pieces that appear here: Rob Filby (through our Obverse collaboration), Liz McGowan and Tigger (collaborations sponsored by the Greenhouse Gallery, Norwich), Mary Mellor (collaboration sponsored by the Norwich 20 Group). And I'm glad for long echoes – resonating still – from Monsanto in Portugal and the generous residency offered me there in 2010 by the University of Coimbra.

For support and encouragement along the way: Nick and Margaret Taylor and my family in Sydney, Judy Chesters, Paeony Lewis, Hannah Stone and (i.m.) Cicely Haines.

This collection was researched and written with the support of a grant from Arts Council England.